Dedication

I cannot say enough about our faith which we have leaned on during times of joy, elation, trouble, doubt, fear and anxiety! No doubt there is a God - one that has everything in His hands. God gave me a husband with whom to travel through life facing our ups and downs together. Mark, you are a true gift. When you are not by my side, I feel a part of me is missing. Marisa, you were the only one that asked me after Decklan was born, "How are you and Mark?" I didn't know then how important that question was. It helped me realize that as a couple whatever we faced we needed to do it side by side.

The prayer support over the years is irreplaceable. Family that loves unconditionally – how wonderful! TA and David, Mom and Dad you are my biggest fans! My "SPRIGS" and "peeps," you are the definition of being loved. You are ones I can look to every day. You know what I am thinking even before I say it! Kelton, my first born who has taught me so much in life; you are my "mighty oak" my gentle giant!

Nate, forever my "study hall buddy," you opened the door for this project and Sandy, a retired teacher but still using your profession in so many ways. You have inspired so many through "TOPS". You have been a blessing helping teach through your editing.

Every Breath You Have Been Given

Tracy L. Burkhart

1999

Revised 2014

Table of Contents

Introduction……………………………………… 6
Decklan's birth/*Every Breath*………………… 8
Days to come……………………………………… 15
On our way home………………………………….. 24
How God prepared the way…………………….. 26
More revelations………………………………. 33
Years following…………………………………. 51
Helpful scripture………………………………… 60

"Sometimes God calms the storms in our lives…

…But sometimes He chooses to calm the Child within the storm"

Introduction

There will be times you stand tall on your mountain top and stretch out your arms holding life at your fingertips - spinning and seeing the world for miles. Joy fills your soul and thoughts of unlimited ability to conquer the world run through your veins. Times will come, however, when you gasp for breath to calm yourself as you fall to your knees helpless in the valley. The challenge is what you will do at each turning point in your life. Who do you run to, who will hold you up and who will lead you on? I have found that life can change in seconds; complete calm can be shattered in a storm that explodes on you in a blink of an eye.

It was a few years after Decklan was born before I was able to write what transpired. I can now see how God was at work beside us the entire time. Some would call these accounts coincidences, but I call them God incidences. Yes miracles still do happen. Decklan has heard us talk often of his "story" and how God saved him for a purpose; but he had never read it until now. God has placed on my heart the need to share now more than ever the miracles that transpired so many years ago.

We were a happy family of three when Mark and I found ourselves expecting our second child. Excitement filled us through the months as we planned ahead. Unfortunately late in my pregnancy, tides began to shift. Prayers started as impromptu ultrasounds indicated that our baby was no longer growing. However, those same ultrasounds did not indicate anything amiss. Little did we know Decklan was already starting to fight for his life while still in my womb. The day would come that would challenge our faith and change our lives forever.

Every Breath You Have Been Given

The relief and amazement of such a miracle filled me as I held my 5lb. 9oz baby boy on July 11, 1995. Delivered twelve days early, Decklan's birth happily caught us by surprise. He had decided it was time to enter the world. He was so tiny, yet so perfect, or so I thought. I held "Decklan T" for mere minutes, looking down at his perfectly shaped nose just like his daddy and holding his bundled warm body. Tears came as I thanked God for a second son. Decklan was the perfect gift to share with my husband on our third wedding anniversary. Mark looked at me with pride and waited patiently for his turn to hold Decklan. I reluctantly handed over our precious, beautiful child and watched as Mark so gently snuggled him close. The nurse quietly intervened and started the normal after birth procedures of cleansing the baby. Mark eagerly carried Decklan to the other room to help.

I lay alone and waited, resting in the peacefulness of the quiet room. However, minutes passed and the quietness began to gnaw at my stomach as no one was returning. Fear crept into my heart. Lying helpless I started to worry and thoughts flashed through my mind. My heart raced, leading to the question, "What's wrong?" Minutes that seemed like hours passed, and no one came into the room. "Where was everyone?" Everything was quiet and still. My face grew hot with anxiety. Finally, Mark confirmed my fears when he walked into the room ever so burdened without our baby.

My entire body filled with a warm dread as I quietly gasped, "Where's our baby?" I held my breath as I waited for an answer. Mark hung his head searching for words. "Something is wrong, and they aren't sure what." He further explained that the nurses were trying to place are our dear little baby boy on an oxygen machine because his oxygen count was very low. They were having issues with the oxygen machine working right. Scared and stunned, I gasped, "I didn't even get to count his fingers and toes." Mark leaned over to hug and comfort me and softly reassured me, "I did. They are all there."

In a dazed silence, we waited. The nurse finally came to transport me to my room. Questions remained unanswered. Mark and I were dazed. We wanted to be able to do something. We wanted everything to be okay. We wanted normal. The nurse reassured us that our family physician, Dr. Beals, had been called. But as time passed and the hour was getting late, she explained their regular procedure. Our doctor was not on call but was alerted, and the physician that was on call was coming in to check on Decklan.

Mark and I looked at each other with no words to define the confusion we both felt. The minutes dragged on as we waited - alone with no answers. Finally anticipation and worry got to the both of us. Mark patiently aided me as I stiffly crawled out of bed and made my way to the nursery to see if there was any news on what was happening.

My eyes passed over the new, snuggled babies each in their own cribs and my eyes rested on a bare, helpless baby laying on a strange piece of equipment. I knew instantly that was Decklan. My vision fogged and my legs weakened as we made our way over to him. The room was strangely quiet; no one said a word. The nurses continued trying to get the oxygen machine to work. Finally a nurse took pity on us and allowed us to touch him but cautioned us not to move him. I wanted to hold Decklan to smother him with love and kisses to promise him this nightmare would be over soon. Tears welled up as I unsteadily leaned against the equipment to touch my helpless son. I felt confused and fear filled my mind. Mark and I were stranded in a room full of worry and anxiety. As I raised my eyes, I saw Dr. Beals making his way to the nursery. In my bewilderment, I realized he must have come on his own accord. Wanting the staff to have adequate freedom to work, we reluctantly moved away.

I felt my legs give way as Mark placed me into a wheelchair and took me back to my room to wait on a report. We sunk in a quiet despair. Time dragged as we waited for answers. What we wanted was reassurance that everything would be okay. Finally with a solemn look, our empathetic doctor came to us calmly suggesting Decklan get immediate care from a specialized facility. He recommended Children's Hospital in Pittsburgh. Dr. Beals further explained that he had heard a slight heart murmur and was a bit concerned.

We readily consented and within an hour the nursery was swarming with a blue uniformed team from Children's. The blackness of time passed, and we again became too anxious to wait for word.

Painfully, I inched myself out of the bed so that Mark and I could search for some answers to our baffling questions.

We walked solemnly to the nursery. The team from Children's busily worked with its own equipment to accommodate our struggling baby. The team doctor met us at the door. He calmly explained the possible scenarios of Decklan's health. I dared not breathe as I listened to every word…he suggested possible undeveloped lungs since he was twelve days early and small, or possibly his heart, or…I heard no more as I collapsed into the chair that was behind me.

"No God, anything but his heart." I felt lost as fear gripped me in this nightmare. My child had looked so perfect hours before with beautiful coloring, shape and form; just small. Could this be? I looked at Mark. He was pale as he took the chair beside me. Silent tears began to fall. We gave our "ok" to transport Decklan to Children's Hospital, and trusted the team to take care of him. Fearing the worst, Mark and I clung to each other as we numbly walked back to my room.

More shocking news followed; we couldn't go with our son. I didn't understand anything. For the first time in my life I was not in control, and I was scared. Shock was taking over this nightmare. Mark made the necessary calls to family updating them and asking for prayer. At 12:30 AM Decklan was wheeled into my room enclosed in a glass "casket." It was a rectangular glass transport case. I stared at his helpless body, I was losing him. Helplessly, we let go of a precious part of our lives we barely knew. The team respectfully waited as we reached out and touched the glass that enclosed our child and looked longingly with silent prayers to God begging Him to intervene. Mark hurried to follow the team outside and watched as the helicopter took flight carrying Decklan away in the darkness of night. Alone again in the hospital room, Mark and I held each other as the convulsions of emotions rocked our bodies.

I had refused any form of medicine until the nurses strongly insisted that I would be of no help to my child unless I rested. Mark went home to pack for our departure in the morning. We would go join Decklan at Children's Hospital after I was discharged. The nurse was to wake me when the doctor called from Children's with a report once Decklan arrived.

I was too distraught to let the sleeping pills take effect. Every phone call that came into the nurse's station would have me at the edge of my bed. By 2 AM my call came. I blindly rushed to the phone.

"Mrs. Burkhart…," the doctor identified himself, there was a long pause, and in a calm voice I heard "…we have a very sick child here." I fought to maintain composure as I held my breath for the ever-important news. He told me that Decklan had a congenital heart defect called "Transposition of the Great Arteries". I felt like a brick wall hit me; "…your child will need heart surgery."

I scrambled to grab a piece of paper at the nurses' station and tried to write all the information down through my tear blurred eyes. I listened as more tears silently slid down my face. I assured the doctor we would be there in the morning as soon as we could and gave him my consent to provide the best care possible in the meantime. I numbly hung up the phone and stumbled to the room to call Mark. Silence filled the phone after I relayed the news to him. Never in our lives had we felt so helpless in a situation.

By 6:30AM the next day, I was showered, dressed and sitting on the edge of the bed after only a few hours of sleep. A nurse just new to her shift walked in, shock and amazement filled her face as I announced I was ready to be discharged as soon as the doctor arrived. I told her that I needed to get to my sick baby. She looked at me wide eyed and quickly exited the room. Apparently, my normally quiet temperament sounded authoritative and firm under the situation at hand.

Minutes later my Dad and our Pastor, Dr. David Holste, stood in our room to give us blessings and prayers before we left. At 7:30 AM Mark and I were on our way to our helpless baby. We arrived at Children's Hospital before 9AM (never to make that good of time traveling in all other years since). I followed Mark as he confidently made his way through the hospital. We were directed to the NICU (Neonatal Intensive Care Unit). Special instructions greeted us, and we complied as we were anxious to see our son. We had to scrub up in a large area of stainless steel sinks. We entered a large room and were then led past rows of babies to the back of a second room.

I had never seen anything like this before. Our little boy lay helpless as hoses and tubes penetrated his body. I gasped at the limp form. So many machines and tubes hooked up to such a small body. I hid my face in Mark's chest as he held me. I wanted to cuddle my baby so badly. Feeling helpless I looked up to the nurse; my only request quietly eased from my lips to just hold my baby for a moment. With a little hesitation and much compassion, she gently maneuvered my arms under his limp form and warned me not to move him at all. Tears blurred my vision and a sob caught in my throat as I felt his tiny warmth fill my arms. Unspoken questions filled my mind. How could this have happened? What were we to do? I took every precaution in pregnancy and was watchful of what I ingested. What was wrong with my baby's heart, so tiny and small?

Days to come…

I never got used to the machinery or the constant alarms on the equipment that was set up to go off at any change or movement in our baby. There were only two hours in the total 24-hour period that we could not be with Decklan in the NICU, and we took advantage of that. Mark and I would take turns sitting by his side as he lay among the many sick children in the hospital rooms - bed after bed of children needing care. I would rub Decklan's feet and hold his little fingers in mine the entire time. We weren't to move him at all. I was so overwhelmed the first night as I stood staring down at him. The helplessness at the situation was numbing. I humbly closed my eyes and truly begged God, "He is your son now, take him and comfort him, I am powerless!" I never realized the power of letting God be in total control until that day. Majestic peace and calm filled my body, and I slowly relaxed allowing my body to rest some and gain strength.

Doctors would come and go and tried to explain the details of what was wrong with Decklan's heart in layman's terms. Simply put, the "plumbing" for his body was backwards. His aorta and pulmonary arteries, the main part of his heart, were backwards. The normal ultrasounds before birth usually check to see if the heart has four chambers and not for other defects. He had all four, but they just happened to be flipped. My heart was heavy in my chest as the doctor further explained that Decklan was living because of a hole in his heart that let the oxygenated blood flow freely, but as that hole naturally closed as he grew, the blood flow to his body would not have oxygen. It was believed to be a heart defect that was caused either by genetics or induced by drug use. Thankfully I knew it wasn't drug abuse on my part, but that didn't clear the guilt of what I might have done that encouraged this defect in my precious baby. The Doctor advised us that if we were to have any other children we could have that issue checked.

There were small dorm type rooms in the basement that were first come first serve for parents not wanting to be too far from their sick child. Somehow just being by Decklan's side, gave us peace that we were helping in some small way. I never looked in the eyes of the other parents as I passed their helpless babies when I made my way through the NICU room to Decklan's side. This seemed to be an unspoken courtesy among the parents; a way to stay composed as much as possible maybe, but it was undeniably an emotional time. I kept my head low to not show the pain and agony I was feeling. Pity was not a feeling you wanted to read in anyone's eyes. Walking past the numerous suffering babies I could not bear to look up and try to offer comfort to others with the comfort and reassurance that I barely grasped myself.

We read all the information we could get our hands on regarding Decklan's heart condition. We were exposed to many terms and definitions with which we were formerly vaguely familiar. They could not switch the heart around due to his "backward plumbing" but they could switch the vessels leading to and from the heart. This type of switch however would leave Decklan with a low pressure valve where we all have high pressure valves holding back the blood flow. This condition could create an enlarged heart due to "back washing" of blood flow. They would actually have to take the heart out of the body as they worked. My mom found comfort in that literature. I cringed at the thought.

The doctors told us a bit about this procedure but stated this type of surgery had been only successful in the United States within just the last ten years and successful in Europe for only the last fifteen years. As far as future prognosis, that information was very limited. The doctor explained it was a condition that caused children to suffocate to death shortly after birth, and that if we looked back on our family trees there may be babies that died early in life that might have had the same undetected disease.

When Decklan was three days old, he underwent an angioplasty/catheterization to help enlarge the hole already there so the blood flow to his body could stay oxygenated, thereby keeping him alive until he was bigger and strong enough for more intensive heart surgery to come. When he was returned to his little corner in the NICU we all prayed for strength for him until his later surgery that was scheduled for July 19th, just eight days after his birth. Mark had to return to work, but was thrilled before he left to experience the first bottle feeding Decklan received at five days old. He was growing stronger thanks to prayers, and we were actually able to feed him and hold him in short increments. His size was still a factor at barely five pounds. I sadly said goodbye to Mark and went to be by Decklan's side. Mark left to go home to be with Kelton and return to work, but would return for Decklan's heart surgery in three days.

I tried to stay with Decklan hourly. He battled jaundice and had a sickly yellow tint to his skin. He was placed under a small glass box with a special light. It seemed they had to change the location of the IV daily. This was routine so not to damage veins, skin, and the fact he was so small. It killed me to walk in and see the needle sticking out of new places on him - his head, neck, foot, or belly button. The sight of the hoses and tubes were never a comfort, they were just a reminder of how sick he really was.

Alone and helpless, I prayed before I left Decklan's side one night from the bottom of my heart. I begged God to give Decklan strength and for God to give him my strength if needed. It seems in our human nature to sometimes resort to the bargaining table with God. It was a desperate prayer of a mother wanting God to protect her son and give him every advantage to life at that instant!

The next morning I awoke early after little sleep as usual and tried to get out of bed. I was faced with the realization that prayers are extremely powerful and that God does hear them. My strength had actually left my body and every joint ached. I was reminded of the prayer I prayed just the night before that God would give Decklan my strength. I know He heard that plea as I could not even physically move my body. Lying flat on my back I wept. Never before that point had I felt such a respect for God and what prayer can do. I thanked God for the realization that He does hear our every prayer. I urged myself up out of the bed after what seemed like hours trying to move my weak limbs and so I could be a physical support by my baby's bedside. Reading books out loud to Decklan or just holding and rubbing his hand or foot was the most I could do to keep reassuring that helpless baby that someone was there for him.

I know God was preparing all those around us to be ready for this birth that would bring many challenges. My parents and sister were able to watch two year old big brother Kelton while I was at the hospital. Mark was working and then traveling back and forth to Pittsburgh. My brother-in-law, David, would return on weekends to help tend to Kelton and his two daughters. My dad was a blessing taking care of the animals we left at home that needed tended and was ever helpful in answering Kelton's questions. An acquaintance at our church called the hospital and offered to mow our grass while we were away and to let us know they were praying. These acts of kindness offered from the heart, touched us.

Not wanting to leave Decklan's side the entire first sixteen days of his life and stay at Children's; I did not sleep many hours or take the time to eat much for breakfast or lunch. I was thankful for our Sunday school class back home that sent a huge brown grocery bag of snacks and goodies, they knew me so well. I lived out of that throughout the stay. Mark's parents lived in the Pittsburgh vicinity and each night they would take us out for dinner and come see Decklan. I didn't want to leave Decklan's side for long but did take that moment to refuel for my laborious waiting.

Blood transfusions were needed to sustain Decklan and I begged the Dr. to use my blood, willing to give all I had to help my struggling child. He assured me that even if I was the same blood type, which I was, that the process was too long and Decklan needed it now - yet another thing out of my control. I conceded and held onto trust and faith that all would be well. My mom did stay with me for a few days while I was alone at the hospital and together we took our turns sitting by Decklan's side praying.

Mark returned and was my silent physical comforter. Our family and pastors were there on the day of Decklan's second major heart surgery. I looked at my mother with pride and admiration as she calmly and gracefully told the surgeon that she was praying for God to work through his hands. I looked at his large calloused hands and compared them to the listless small tiny child and knew it was up to God to proceed. I could not do another thing.

It was a long 8 1/2 hours of waiting during our infant's tedious surgery. Children's Hospital said they only did about 15 of the Transposition of the Great Artery surgeries each year on young babies, and that was if they could catch their heart defect in time.

All the materials and pamphlets I had read, did not prepare me for Decklan's distorted body laying in front of me in the PICU (Pediatric Intensive Care Unit) recovery room. My child once so tiny and frail was bloated past recognition, and my eyes shifted to the one large tube emanating from his chest. The chest tube leaked fluid of all colors from Decklan's body. Decklan's sternum had to be cut and pulled apart for them to get to his tiny heart. Tape covered the line of stitches down his chest after they sewed and wired him back into place. I didn't know how or when this nightmare would end for us. I did however keep my prayers flowing towards Heaven begging for this to end and Decklan to be healthy and at home. With my hands tied and helpless, I was brought to my grounded faith; the only hope on which I could hold.

In the days following this surgery, Decklan recovered very quickly. I spent all my waking hours by his side, I prayed, contemplated life, and felt like the movie screen was playing in front of me with the script unknown. Because Decklan recovered so quickly, he was moved to his own room within two weeks of his hospital stay and after only a few days after his heart repair. Mark yet again returned home to continue working and to be with big brother Kelton. I was scared of the responsibility of caring for Decklan. I was alone with my child who had wire sticking out of his chest, "just in case" the nurse said, in case of what? Needless to say, I was filled with fear. During his first hours and days of life, he sustained by monitors and machines with nurses around the clock. Now he was on his own without continual monitoring. Was he ready? Was I ready?

The time had come then for the nurse to remove the last wires that were in Decklan's chest. Nothing prepared me for the sleeping child, who was fighting to regain his strength, to be wakened so abruptly by the removal of these foreign objects. His body had already started incorporating the wires into his healing flesh. This flesh was ripped as the wires were removed. The cries of pain from Decklan will ever be etched on my brain and in my heart as the wires slowly came out of his body.

It was the last straw. A sob caught in my throat as I exited the hospital. The stress of the past two weeks mounted. I had ignored my emotional and physical needs, and it was time to take care of myself. I was in need of an escape. I tried to walk off my extra energy outside in downtown Oakland. I found myself walking into a hair salon, sitting in the chair, and saying, "Give me something different, I need a change- a new me". I watched as both girls exchanged looks in the mirror as I gave the brief rundown of the past day's events. Layers of ten inches or more of hair began to fall covering the floor. Little did I know the outside care and grooming, though important, didn't compare to the major work being formed on the inside of my heart, of compassion, giving, and trusting the importance of prayer.

After returning to the hospital, I wanted held and comforted as I sat alone in the hospital room with Decklan. I picked up the phone to call Mark and asked him to come back to the hospital earlier than he had planned and be with me, but there was no answer. I buried my face on the sheets next to Decklan as he lay quietly in the hospital bed. I begged for some relief, comfort and control. I was at my breaking point. Many times I reminded God, "Okay I think this is enough, not sure I can handle more". God knew I needed someone physical to reassure me that life would once again be normal. I missed my joy and sunshine of strength, Kelton. I needed something familiar and stable, something I was sure of, life as I knew it.

Not even a half hour later, Mark walked through the room to surprise me. I hugged him with relief, not wanting to let go. I prayed and tried to trust. God knew what I needed at that moment, and He was working ahead when He sent Mark to be by my side. I was scared of not only what was happening around me but also of my emotional change. I was always in control, so I thought, until now.

I realized that it was God who is to be in control, and we are to listen, learn, and lean on Him.

On the way home and looking back to God's preparation…

I was at the hospital sixteen days with Decklan. I clung to the memory of a sermon heard years previous that God would not give us more than we can handle. A couple of times, I unnecessarily reminded God that I did think I was at my limit.

We left the hospital with a 5lb 2oz-baby boy that July of 1995. The last sobs of relief, pity, sorrow, and confusion exited my body for a major part of the way home. I could finally hold my baby boy and show my love to him; if only I didn't worry about undoing what the doctors had done. Afraid to move him much for the first days home, Decklan just lay in our arms. Looking down at the tiny form, it seemed his entire leg was only the size of my thumb.

He slept many of his first few months at home. Pictures were hard to get taken at a professional location. We would wait in line and then when it came our turn, he would be sleeping and we would be refused photos due to store policy of not taking pictures of a sleeping baby because I was told they looked like funeral pictures. Due to lack of energy and will, I did not fight. I shook my head and left thinking, if you only knew how close we were, you would not even make such a comment.

I would constantly compare Decklan's growth with many baby books to make sure he was developing correctly and timely. Every milestone of rolling over, sitting up, talking, walking was an assurance that he was progressing in normal development. In the back of my mind, was worry of such trauma having an effect on his cognitive development. In weak moments, fear and doubt entered in my thoughts. How could I protect Decklan from life's adventures that lay ahead of him? I have learned that it is not I protecting him but his heavenly Father.

Reflection of how God prepared the way...

Years later I realize my relationship with the Lord has grown by great lengths. I never ask "why" when I look at Decklan and his scarred chest. "Thank You" is more on my thoughts of how blessed with him we are. I learned in those sixteen days at the hospital that God provides, strengthens, and comforts in His own miraculous ways. We look back and know God was there preparing us for Decklan's birth, held us up during it, and continues to be with us each step of the way. Some people would call the events that fell into place with Decklan's birth, merely coincidence. I call it our wonderful Father taking matters into His own hands. Health insurance for our family started eleven days before Decklan was born. The day of my regular routine doctor's appointment, and day of Decklan's birth, it happened that my girlfriend, Aunt Brennie, had to work and was not able to walk Kelton around the mall, (their special routine during my pregnancy checkups). Instead, Kelton was already safe at my mom and dad's home, and starting his extended stay with family.

That day Decklan was born, I felt no labor pains. It was twelve days before his actual due date. At that regular appointment the doctor sent me to the hospital right away stating that I was in labor. I really doubted the doctor because I felt nothing out of ordinary. I had given birth before, and I thought I would definitely know if I was in labor. However, the only way the doctor would let me drive out of the office was with the promise I would go get my husband to drive me to the hospital. I did stop by Mark's place of work and told him not to worry about coming with me, and that I didn't feel any different. Little did I know, I was actually in labor and our baby was soon to arrive. The doctor was right. I dread to think of being home alone with dear two year old Kelton while giving birth so unexpectedly to a very sick child. I was thankful that birthing was fast, and I was able to avoid any drugs that inevitably could have affected Decklan's already existing poor condition. It also helped me in my recovery so that I could be in Pittsburgh.

Decklan needed checked and the nurse was confident that the physician on call could take care of matters. Strangely, out of the blue, late at night, Dr. Beals decided to come and check out Decklan's situation. Did he feel a prompting of his spirit to come in? I am sure God had a bit to do with the fact that he came walking into the hospital so late at night. He was the only local doctor who heard a slight murmur of the heart alerting us to the fact Decklan needed special attention right away.

The list continues. It all transpired during the summer months where my mom was off of school for summer break, and my sister was free to leave her home with her young girls to take care of my two year old son. They made it possible for me to stay at the hospital the entire time with Decklan. I praise God I was a stay at home mom who worked out of the home and able to drop everything to stay by the side of my baby boy struggling for his life. To me these were not coincidences but the hand of God.

God is in control of our lives and knows what lies ahead -paving the way for events to fall into place. I praise God for the honor of His presence in our lives. My faith has never been this strong, and now I know the extreme power of prayer. The memory of me lying in my bed, my strength gone and, recalling the prayer I had prayed the night before for God to use my strength for my son, will remind me for years to come that God does hear our prayers. Bargaining as I had done is not recommended because God is a big God. He can handle any situation and He doesn't need my strength, but I feel at that moment it was more important for Him to let me know He did hear me and was right by my side. It resulted in me realizing I could lean on Him in any time of need.

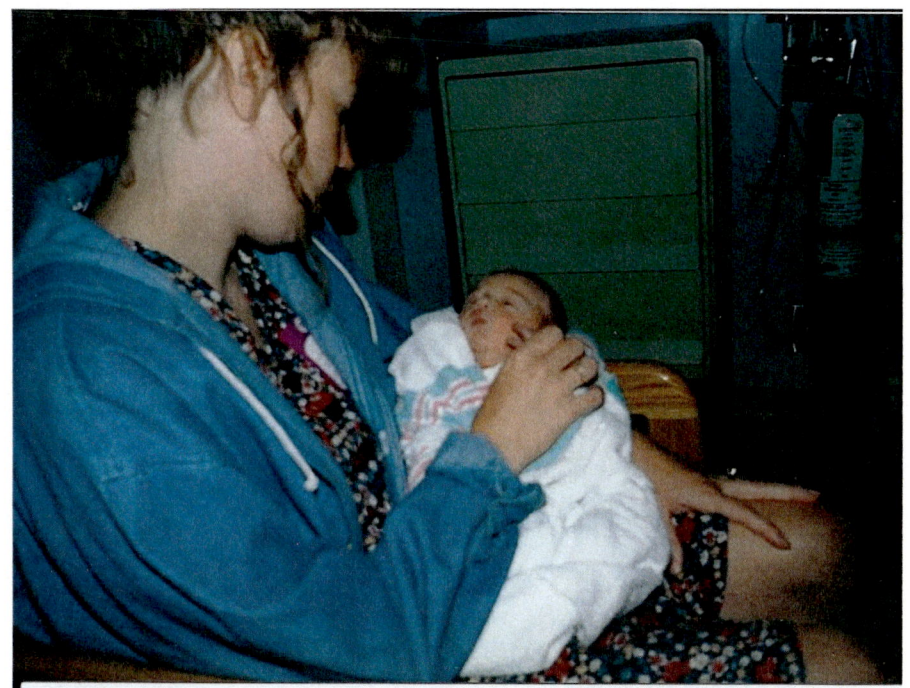

Figure 1: Decklan a few weeks old finally off machines and relieved of tubes and IV's with mother Tracy

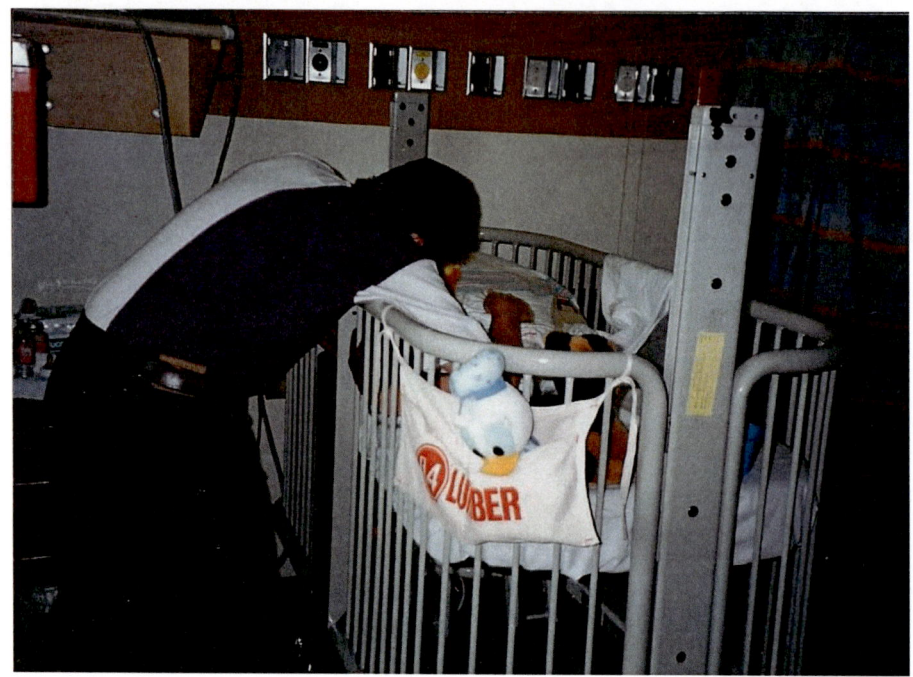

Figure 2: Mark with Decklan 14 days old at Children's (Mark's job at the time was at 84 Lumber, hence the work apron)

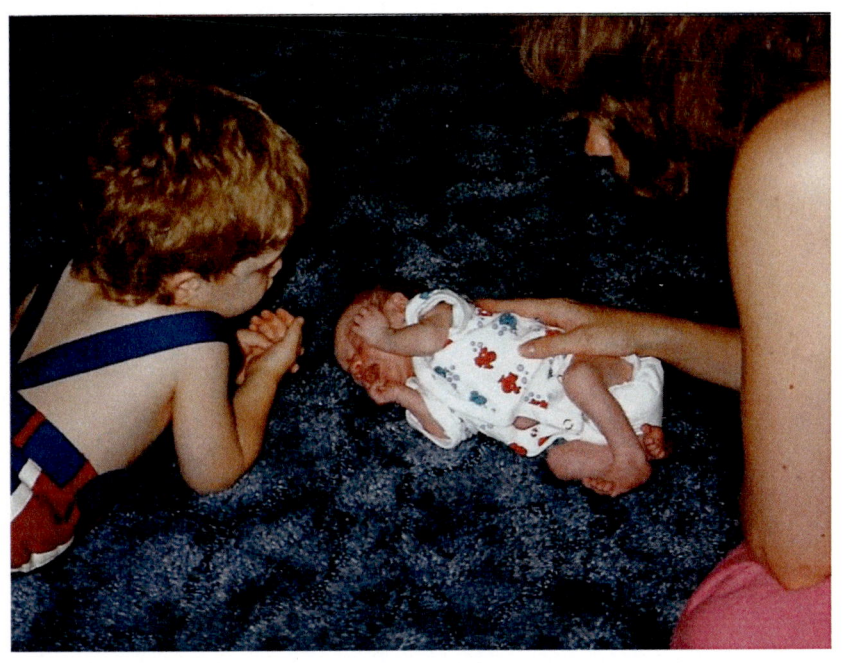

Figure 3: First day home with Decklan, 16 days old.

Kelton 2 1/2 yrs and Tracy

Figure 4: Kelton (age 2) with Great Grandma Ray and Decklan (within 1 month of being home)

More revelations about how God worked on Decklan's behalf…

As we watched Decklan grow, we saw how God was giving us a glimpse into His wondrous work in our everyday lives. No doubt there were many challenges and worries with Decklan's condition. He will always be limited on medicine he can take, so we battled many years with horrible ear infections. Once he even dealt with a burst ear drum due to restrictions on decongestants. Years later he was strong enough to finally get tubes in his ears that helped with the constant infections. Yet, Decklan never let his limitations affect his quality of mindset and desire to love life.

In spite of Decklan's medical problems, he grew and progressed cognitively. We look back to when Decklan was very young and learning to talk and remember it strange that Decklan would have a different language at times that we just didn't understand. We just passed it off as "baby talk", but we noticed some other odd happenings. Decklan would be playing by himself, and we would find him talking to someone in this "baby talk" as if they were right there beside him. We thought nothing of it; he was learning to speak and it was just gibberish, we first thought. We teased Decklan after seeing him talk to a "friend" we could not see. He actually would focus on something intently and wave and talk often. A bit amazed, we passed it off as a child's imagination At one point Mark and I moved away for Mark's employment. My sister and I asked Decklan, "Did your friend ride in the moving van with us?" Decklan looked at us as if we were crazy and simply said, "of course not, he flew behind us". I started to take special interest in these "conversations" thereafter.

It became second nature for me to find Decklan talking to his "friend" in his special language. I once asked him what his "friend" looked like and where he usually saw this "friend". He simply explained that his friend often stood at the end of his bed in long white clothing. Decklan said he had long hair and a sword. There was no way he could have gotten these images from books or media of any sort. Both boys were too young yet. I understand now as I read in the bible of how Mary "pondered" things. Yes I pondered these things and the information Decklan shared with the innocence and truth of a child. Oh, how wonderful to see a child's faith and to see through a child's eyes. I am sure Decklan was guarded by an angel, this special "friend" that he talked to and saw often in his everyday world. I treasure the thought of God sending a special angel to stand guard over Decklan. Looking back, God was ever present, ever real, ever there for all of us and continues to be. For that I will be forever thankful.

My relationship with God is forever expanding in our everyday trials. Decklan's story continued to grow in our hearts and minds, and puzzle pieces we didn't even know were missing, seem to piece together.

At the age of four I once again called desperately on God to touch Decklan. Stricken with sickness that wouldn't leave his body; I laid my hands on his head and prayed in Jesus' name. Decklan stopped me midstream as I was praying, "Jesus take Decklan..." He grabbed my hand and said, "Don't pray that way; I don't want to go with Jesus now". I was taken aback and reassured him that this is how Jesus taught us to pray for the sick. I continued explaining that Jesus hears our prayers and heals us and that there was nothing to fear. Decklan quickly said, "I know, I know". Not knowing exactly what he knew as a four year old, I somewhat impatiently said, "How do you know?" Not expecting his answer in the least he simply replied, "<u>When I was in the arms of Jesus at the doors of heaven.</u>" Stunned, I quickly questioned him..."What?" Very matter of fact, like I should have known when this was, he responded, <u>"When there was two of me."</u> I gulped those words down, too stunned to respond. I realized something miraculous had happened. Careful not to lead Decklan on, I composed myself and quietly asked when this was. My precious four year old turned in my arms and said, "<u>When they cut me!</u>" He made slicing motions down his chest with his hand. Tears filled my eyes as the shock set upon me of what he was saying. We had never explained the process of his heart surgery to him, or what they had to do to him when he was a tiny baby. I silently relished this revelation and praised God for His tangible comfort to my son. This type of spiritual interaction I had read about, but never dreamed I would be so close to someone who had experienced it.

The excitement of this event I will hold close to my heart forever! Four and half years after struggling through Decklan's heart surgery, God revealed to me through a small child, that when a child of

His is hurting, He is there. I prayed helplessly on July 12, 1995 to Jesus, "...He is your son now, I am helpless, take him, he's yours". I believe in all my heart that what Decklan revealed to me was that Jesus did take him and comfort him. I am blessed entirely by Decklan's birth and surgery and feel closeness to God like I never had before.

A few years after Decklan's birth, I struggled with emotions in writing the events of his entrance into the world and his surgery. I would have never guessed that 4 1/2 years later Decklan would add another chapter to his own story. I never look back and ask why anymore; I just smile with the knowledge that through Decklan's birth and surgery, we were blessed beyond imagination. Jesus cared and loved us enough to <u>hold</u> and comfort my baby boy in <u>His very arms</u>. Some critics might discredit Decklan's story of Jesus at Heaven's doors to a lively imagination, but I do not believe that a four year old would be able to create such facts. I credit it fully to our comforter and healer, Jesus. *"I tell you the truth, unless you change and become like little children, you will never enter the kingdom of heaven." Matthew 18:3*

Shortly after Decklan shared his interaction with our Lord, I shared Decklan's revelation with some family and close friends. Not many choose to share something so strange and out of ordinary for fear of being looked at as crazy or eccentric. I treasured the thought of Jesus caring enough about a simple little family and child, to come and hold him in His arms. That is my Lord I have come to know, caring about each and every one of us. We are His family and children, we are daughters and sons of a King, and He does hear our every prayer and plea.

Another of God's provisions came through a conversation with my aunt who lives in Florida. She has a nursing background and always asked for a health update on Decklan; I said I would love to find his original doctor who was so kind and skilled if ever Decklan needed additional surgeries. She inquired a bit more, and I casually told her the name of the doctor and that he had moved from Children's. She got a strange amazed look on her face and exclaimed that she knew the doctor- that in fact he worked at her same facility. Really, I thought? Why do we doubt at times that God had this in His hands- that He has a plan. He will provide comfort and we just need to trust and believe!

One of the most important messages we left the hospital with from this doctor was to treat Decklan as a normal child. He cautioned us to not baby him or treat him special, to raise him just as if he was a normal little boy. Mark and I tried to follow that advice when raising our boys. Early on in the brothers' relationship I realized we were doing a good job of trying to follow that advice when Decklan came quietly and hesitant to me after a bath night. He was very concerned for his brother Kelton. He actually wanted to know why Kelton did not have two belly buttons; he wanted to know what was wrong with Kelton. I was taken aback for a moment and realized that Decklan thought something was wrong with Kelton because his chest and belly did not look like his. Decklan didn't think anything was wrong with him but worried for his brother. I hugged him and laughed at the reality of what he thought and explained that no, it actually was not what was wrong with either but that the extra little "art work" of scars on Decklan was because his heart had to have some work . The extra belly button just happened to be from where he had his chest tube after surgery. He wasn't sure how to take this information, and I am sure he still wondered in his younger child's mind why everyone's chest didn't look like his.

It wasn't long after this that Decklan shared yet another story of being at the "doors of Heaven". I had been working selling Tupperware during the nights and through a promotion and challenge, I had won this trip to Disney world. What a blessing! We had never gone on a family vacation of this extent. This would be the boys' first experience flying! As the jet took off, Mark and I just sat back and enjoyed their facial expressions and excitement. At one moment as Decklan was looking out the window as the plane went up and up and up, he exclaimed in such excitement as he stared out amongst the clouds, "We are almost to the doors of Heaven!" Mark and I looked at each other and said not a word; we just felt contented and amazed. We held in our hearts the hope and truth in his statement that we were close to the wonderful doors of Heaven.

You know, I now think and find it odd that Decklan never said "gates" of Heaven. Is it because as a young child with limited vocabulary that he only recognized those "gates" as a type of door?

We might not ever know the answer to some of these questions, but I will treasure the reflections that Decklan shared with us so many years ago, and I praise our Lord for His protection and care for our very sick child.

There has been worry and fears at different times of Decklan's health - there were times when his body just didn't keep up with his everyday living and playing. I would often walk into the house or in a room looking for Decklan because I didn't hear him playing, and I would find him slumped over a pile of toys or stack of books. My breath would catch in my throat. I would race to him, lift him up and cradle him in my arms to see if he was actually still breathing. We received notice from Children's that some patients who received blood transfusions during the dates Decklan was at the hospital, could have gotten a bad batch of blood. We had to go through additional testing to make sure Decklan was not exposed. It took years for me not to get an instant physical sickness in the pit of my stomach at the sound of a helicopter. The sound was like a knife stabbing my heart, transporting me back to the moments of helplessness agony in memory of Decklan's first moments of life.

These continual scares started to affect my mental health. I would be awakened nights just having a dream of being at Decklan's funeral, with the taunting question of what would I say at his funeral? Fearful of these morbid dreams, I would pray for relief. I would have lengthy conversations with God in the middle of sleepless nights, until I finally found peace. It was as if God was saying, look at Decklan, and look at how he enjoys life with every breath. I concluded that yes indeed Decklan did live every moment of life happy and full of life.

Decklan celebrated every breath with the joy and elation of living in the moment. He never complained, never cried or fussed. He loved life. I studied him daily and realized he was such a happy child that he didn't waste moments on worry or fear. This child of poor health and young years was teaching me the importance of life. He taught me not to waste a moment of letting "life" get you down; to enjoy and be happy at each moment; to live life as it truly is, a blessing, a gift. Sleep started then to fill my nights. I was comforted in that gift and answer right in front of me, the example of contentment in my small child.

Figure 5: Kelton 3 1/2 yrs and Decklan 16 months old

A Child's Faith

"Jesus loves me, this I know
For the Bible tells me so"
Little children ask no more,
For love is all they're looking for,
And in a small child's shining eyes
The faith of all the ages lies.

And tiny hands and tousled heads
That kneel in prayer by little beds
Are closer to the dear Lord's heart
And of His kingdom more a part
Than we who search, and never find,
The answers to our questioning mind.

For faith in things we cannot see
Requires a child's simplicity
For, lost in life's complexities,
We drift upon uncharted seas
And slowly faith disintegrates
While wealth and power accumulate.

For the more man learns, the less he knows,
And the more involved his thinking grows
And, in his arrogance and pride,
No longer is man satisfied
To place his confidence and love
With childlike faith in God above.

O Father, grant once more to men
A simple childlike faith again
And, with a small child's trusting eyes,
May all men come to realize
That faith alone can save man's soul
And lead him to a higher goal.

Helen Steiner Rice **

** "Used with permission of the Helen Steiner Rice Foundation, Suite 2100, Atrium Two, 221 East Fourth Street, Cincinnati, Ohio 4502."

Figure 6: Spring 2003, Decklan 7 1/2 ready for baseball!

Figure 7: Fall of 2003, Decklan 8 yrs with friends on his favorite horse Maggie

Figure 8: 2005 at Home Depot, Decklan (10yrs) with mom Tracy

Figure 9: 2008 Decklan (13 1/2) with Grampy Ray

Figure 10: Mt. Rushmore, SD 2009 Decklan (14), Mark, Tracy and Kelton (16)

Figure 11: Fall 2010 Decklan (15 1/2) Varsity Golf, 9th grade

Figure 12: Decklan (15) at Grandparent Burkhart's lake cottage; Canadohta Lake- Union City, Pa

Figure 13: Family mission trip~ Appalachian Service Project; Decklan(16) with Mark and Tracy and cousin Tara

Years Following…

Years have flown by and we awake to blessings every day. Decklan has grown into a handsome young man. Graduation and college for Business Management are in his plans. His love of history continues and love for golf will always be a part of him. Most importantly, we believe with all our hearts that he has a mission, a purpose. He just needs to let God lead him and direct him.

Decklan enjoys the gift of the great outdoors: hunting, shooting, fishing, boating, creating and designing projects for his Jeep. He fills his summers with working at Seneca Hills, a local church camp, and expanding his "Faith Walk". He works at the local sporting goods store which opens doors for him to enjoy all the sports no matter his health limitations.

Kelton had a responsibility of being a gentle older brother from the day we brought Decklan home. He had to learn early on to restrain himself from normal rough-housing. Now these brothers share a love of outdoors and vehicle puttering and fixing.

There were times of anxiety when the yearly heart checks ups would come and results would show an increase in the leaking valve and an enlarged heart, but prayers and putting our faith forward kept us going. Annually Decklan has an EKG and an echocardiogram done to check his heart.

He has had challenges of migraine headaches for which he can only take limited medicine to help with pain and daily herbal supplements that are heart friendly. He still has a scar on the side of his neck where an IV was placed. I look at it and I remember fully back to his helpless body with needles and hoses of all sorts 'plugged' into him to keep him alive.

It has been sad and discouraging over the years to watch other kids put all their energy into sports in which Decklan wanted to participate. He watched his brother play football and held his head high knowing he would never give nor take that crushing blow in the field of action. He has watched as friends raced back and forth on the basketball court and cheered them on, knowing deep down he could not keep up that kind of competitive pace. He saw weights of huge proportion waiting to be lifted but knew if he dared he might collapse under the lack of function of his heart.

Decklan carries this knowledge daily and has learned to embrace what he can do and to enjoy the task. No one is stopping him from enjoying the life he has been given, he can still sling his kayak over his shoulders, ride the whitewater in Ohio, or climb to the mountain top in Yellowstone. He might have a few limitations, but he takes what he can do and fills that with all his energy. He has fully embraced what he can do with being part of many clubs and groups in school such as Varsity Club for Golf and Track N Field, National Honor Society and others. He has gone to Districts twice for Golf and made it to the Regional rounds twice.

He was a part of a team that attended state level competitions for the Envirothon- an academic game based in life sciences/conservation.

Decklan's grandma – my mom, taught me all my life to count my blessings no matter the situation. She has been and still is an example of strength of mind and soul. No doubt we have found ourselves in many valleys during life. We do not dwell in the caves; we sit in the valleys beside the flowing stream of water watching the current flow over the rocks reaching out to catch the sunshine's warmth! I have tried to pass that on to Decklan and Kelton. There is a purpose, a plan, a destiny put in place for each of our lives!

I sit nineteen years later, we are still traveling the same roads home from the hospital. I look back at my now grown boy, who still has an unknown path ahead in life. I reflect and realize how time has passed. No longer do I need to stand beside the bedside and help hold Decklan in place on the echocardiogram table. His over six foot frame now hangs over the edge. He no longer is snuggled in his car seat but fills the backseat.

I reflect upon the last news from the heart doctor. Decklan's has moderate to severe aortic insufficiency. His left ventricle is currently moderately dilated with low-normal systolic function. This basically is a condition of a weakened aortic valve letting the blood flow and backwash into the left ventricle, resulting in an enlarged heart. It isn't holding the blood back like it should in normal function of the heart. To maintain his heart the healthiest, an increase of medicine was called for. With the maximum dose of medicine, the doctor was hopeful it would lessen the pressure of blood flow and help the leaking aortic valve. There is a chance however that a valve replacement will be considered. Due to Decklan's heart being backwards, his aortic valve is a low pressure valve trying to keep up with a high pressure valve job. A stress test will follow with a complete team of adult heart cardiologists to determine the next step for Decklan to help him maintain a healthy heart. Years ago, when we knew a valve replacement was a possible challenge for Decklan, I silently requested from God to let Decklan be full grown when we would have to face this. Replacement valves do not grow with a growing body. Now that we are there and Decklan is full grown, I want to change my silent request; "God, may he not have to have a valve replacement at all!" A friend has often reminded me, "Be careful what you pray for". I see we tend to limit God in what we consider humble prayer requests. I want to be bold and ask God for a complete healing for Decklan. You could join me in that prayer!

Decklan realizes that with limitations also come challenges to meet each day with new hope and expectation. He longingly looks at his close friends as they enter into the military. He is red, white and blue at heart with patriotism in his blood. He has in the family bloodline many who have served Army, Air Force, Navy, even a Flying Tiger- George Burgard. His heart condition limits his career choices, naturally causing doubt about decisions ahead. We do have a hand in our destiny, with the choices we make and paths we take; but belief and trust brings us to our Lord for leading. God has created us for His purpose. I remember sitting with Decklan in his room after a downhearted conversation filled with doubt and lost hope; I said, "Decklan you were created for a reason, God saved you so many years ago for a purpose!" Figuring out that purpose is the challenge before him. He might have health limitations, but he has blessings before him and is alive. Every morning we wake up to a new sunrise, a new fresh start, a new hope!

It is our choice of what we do with that "hope". Do we look at it as a blessing? Every breath we breathe, we have been given! Realizing this gift and embracing it might just be a great way to start the day!

Figure 14: Christmas 2013, Kelton, Anna, Mark, Tracy, Decklan, and Rogi Bear (Oh, and Decklan's Jeep)

Figures 15: Cranberry High School Graduation 2014 pictures...

Scriptures that I have favored and leaned on often:

"So do not fear, for I am with you; do not be dismayed, for I am your God. I will strengthen you and help you; I will uphold you with my righteous right hand." Isaiah 41:10 (NIV)

"Those who hope in the Lord will renew their strength. They will soar on wings like eagles; they will run and not grow weary, they will walk and not be faint." Isaiah 40:31 (NIV)

"Be joyful always; pray continually, give thanks in all circumstances, for this is God's will for you in Christ Jesus."

1 Thessalonians 5:16-18 (NIV)

"Trust in Him at all times O people; pour out your hearts to Him, for God is our refuge" Psalm 62:8 (NIV)

"But the Lord is faithful and He will strengthen and protect you from the evil one" 2 Thessalonians 3:3 (NIV)

Psalm 91……..Entire chapter is wonderful chapter for protection

"Do not let the sun go down while you are still angry, and do not give the devil a foothold" Ephesians 4:26-27

"Do not be anxious about anything, but in everything, by prayer and petition, with thanksgiving, present your requests to God. And the peace of God, which transcends all understanding, will guard your hearts and your minds in Christ Jesus." Philippians 4:6-7

"I can do everything through Him who gives me strength." Philippians 4:13

"...we also rejoice in our suffering, because we know that suffering produces perseverance; and perseverance, character; and character, hope. And hope does not disappoint us, because God has poured out his love into our hearts by the Holy Spirit, whom he have given us. Romans 5:3-5

"Cast all your anxiety on Him because He cares for you"

1Peter 5:7

One of Decklan's favorite:

"Cast your cares on the Lord and he will sustain you, He will never let the righteous fall" Psalm 55:22

Scripture touches your heart and sometimes that is all you have to cling to. They are promises from God. His word is a word of comfort, not just written for years ago, but for now and always to be written on our hearts! If you have any doubt of a superior being, an Ultra God that created all and has all, let me assure you there is one! What do you have to lose to check it out? To lean in and trust the hope that is offered in everyday living. I know the ups and downs in life leave you feeling like a train wreck or like it is hopeless. I promise you there will still be ups and downs, but I also promise you that you don't have to ever do it alone. Life takes time; we will have lists of things of worries and concerns that we want taken care of or fixed right away. There will be prayers not answered in life. Bargains made with God only to feel your heart and soul torn when we don't get our request. Notice I said, "Our requests". Prayer for healing sometimes doesn't come in the way we expect. Our prayers are not always answered the way we think they should be. Sometimes we are called to wait in our delay. Trust and faith is questioned. It is a daily walk of faith and relationship with God. One thing I can tell you is that God is forever by your side. In life we will hurt, we will scar, we will doubt and throw a fit or two, but always walking beside us is GOD! Decklan's story gives many examples of God interacting in our lives. God provided His presence when we didn't even realize He was there. He acted before we even knew what we needed. Looking back it is easy to see Him right there with us in many ways. His ways are better than our ways at times.

"Trust in the Lord with all your heart and lean not on your own understanding; in all your ways acknowledge Him and He will make your paths straight."   *Proverbs 3:5-6*

Prayers for Decklan will continue. God wants him well. Jesus awoke healing as a big ministry of the Christian Church. Healings can be in different forms however. It can be miraculous, gradual, or even coping with your condition. I never doubt God hearing our requests for healing for Decklan. There is a purpose in all we have experienced. God will be glorified in any "cross" we are asked to bear. However, never discount the complete ability for Him to heal you in any way you ask.

Times will require us to wait during our 'life storms'. In the waiting, bitterness, anger and doubt can grow. It is your choice to turn those unproductive reactions into growth. Growth of grace or compassion towards others, growth in relationship with God, and growth as a hopeful human being extending love in your waiting. "Oh but I have done too much in the past, I am not sure I deserve my prayers to be answered"…have you said that? How can a true, good God, want to hear from me? Stained beyond stained I am. Newsflash, those sitting in the pews of the Church, those preaching, all have a past of stains. Hypocrites are all that fill the pews of church you say, well you know what; they are sinners that is all. They are searching for a path, truth and answers to life cries of help. They have just admitted it and are searching.

You don't usually go to the doctor's office if you aren't sick, church helps keep Christians grounded and keeps them on the path they are searching for. They are there waiting for God to lead them.

When you feel desperate and life is closing in around you, or you are confused and not sure which way to go, know simply there is a way. A way for a better life and I challenge you to try it, what do you have to lose? You can grasp onto a real source of comfort in your time of need and a peace that gets you through the hard times. You don't have to walk alone in your worries or troubles. Put it to the test, is God real? If you are an unbeliever a simple prayer such as this; "Jesus I know I am a sinner, forgive my sins (Romans 3:23, 1 John 1:9), I need a savior (Romans 6:23, John 3:16), please come into my heart and make me new in YOU (Revelation 3:20)". Simple but so extravagant in what Jesus can do for you, wait and trust, continue to confess your sins and get in the Bible to read and see for yourself what the blessings God has waiting for you. He will act and He will move, so get ready for Him to show up!

Contact me tlbheartbeat@gmail.com and I will pray for you, I don't have all the answers to life but I do have a heart for Jesus, and He will show Himself to you, there is hope.

About the Author

I never dreamed how rewarding being a mom could be. God graced Mark and me with two handsome boys, (what mother wouldn't say that about her own?). The entire school years of the boys I had the pleasure to work around all their schedules, so I could be there for them. I worked many different jobs from home. Faith and family were first on my heart and many sacrifices were made so we could make that work. We face life together and walk through struggles with each ones' support. I have prayed now in this stage in the boy's life that God will lead them each to a special lady to spend the rest of their lives with.

We have gone on many mission trips together as a family, and I hope each boy has it written on his heart the love of serving our Lord in the areas He has planned for them. Kelton and Decklan both are gifted in different areas and I already see how God can use them. My husband and I plan to expand our mission outreach to Africa soon. It also has been laid on our hearts to help with disaster relief. After prayer to God saying, put me somewhere where you can use me Lord and where I can save funds to help us help others; I have currently found myself in a local school classroom as an aide. I have been blessed to work many various jobs over the years; having a degree in Speech Communications and Public Relations, has trained me well for versatility.

I also have a minor in Art, so my love of nature and the beauty comes naturally. Artistically I love to capture nature with photos, art and painting; creating with my hands and enjoying the majesty of it all!

I have begun illustrating for a few different books, one of which is in print; check it out; <u>'Tommy the Tortoise's Wish for Speed'</u> by Nathan Mercer.

I will continue to live each day looking for the blessings around me in a sometimes sad, unthankful world. Sometimes staying positive and holding onto my beliefs, is all the hope that will get me to the next day, the promise of walking through the storms of life, for the next new adventure and challenge. I have strived to extend "grace" and "joy" to all those who I meet! Life is short, breath the fresh breath of each new sunrise to fulfill your purpose in life…………..You all have one!!!!!!!!

FAITH

When you come to the edge of all the light you have known and are about to step out into the darkness, faith is knowing one of two things will happen…there will be something to stand on or you will be taught how to fly.

Made in the USA
Middletown, DE
11 December 2014